MW00789632

# The Emerging Self

Copyright © 2009 Anne DiDomenico
All rights reserved.
ISBN: 1-4392-3239-3
EAN-13: 978-1439232392

Visit www.booksurge.com to order additional copies.

# The Emerging Self
## The Inner Bridge Home

Anne DiDomenico

# Dedication

*To all who………….*

*…………………….seek the Light*

*………....…..find the Light...*

*….…..KNOW the Light*

*WE WALK AS ONE*

## ACKNOWLEDGEMENT

*Deep gratitude to Les*

*my perfect partner in this adventure*

*of expanding consciousness*

*and Self-realization*

## THE EMERGING SELF

The Emerging Self…
waits with all patience
for silence to fill the moment….

so the sound barrier of your thoughts
may be broken just long enough
for Its Voice to be heard.

This Voice sounds different
if you listen…..…..

quiet, gentle…
It cannot be heard
in the midst of fear…
unless you choose to hear it…

It speaks to the extent you allow.

It's very presence…
if you were to observe it…
would be radiant and e x p a n s I v e
glorious and beyond extraordinary.
This…is who you truly are.

Understand what it means
to choose love in every moment…
to live in the N O W
with no past or future in mind…

Understand what this means
and you take the first steps
in merging what appear to be
contradictory parts of yourself.

*These parts are really
your conflicting thoughts
out-of-sync with your heart
seeking resolution in your mind.*

*As this merging takes place,
your true Self begins to emerge*

*and your capacity to extend love expands
while you slip back less and less
into old habits of thought.*

*As you stay the course…
and remain firm in your resolve…*

*the beautiful Self that you are
expresses through the body
in ever greater measure…
for longer periods of "time"…
until you no longer reside in "time."*

*Once fully awakened in the Self,
you come to the realization that…*

**YOU ARE THE SELF
YOU HAVE AWAKENED TO.**

*By the gift of Grace,
you have awakened your self
to the truth of who you are.*

*When this miracle occurs…*

*the journey is complete…*

*for the Emerging Self*

*remembers It-Self*

*as the ONE*

*Now.*


*Welcome Home*

# Introduction/Foreword

*The writings in this volume came to be thru the inspiration of the moment….. what I call listening to the Voice within. We all have it. The Voice is the' ways and means' for coming Home, and these words describe the inner bridge I've walked… motivated by the deepest desire and intent to live the dream of merging with my Highest SELF: to shift from knowing my 'self' as the small "i" identified with a body… to knowing my 'self' as awakened and in remembrance of who I truly am.*

*Full emergence of the SELF is possible when we hold intent and desire for it, yet so often, life appears to be a running collection of events and experiences where the only use of time is in getting through whatever is happening and living the status quo. Time spent in silence…in a quiet space with our selves…away from the pushing and pulling of the world… is given minimal thought at best.*

*It has been my practice over the years to increasingly honor time alone as a way to hear what is truly going on within me. Because of this choice, I 'heard' amazing words that inspired me to continue on when all seemed lost. In this way, I came to know a peace that surpasses any list I might have created as criteria for gaining peace.*

*The Voice of our Inner Authority is ever present and ready to guide us if we but open our hearts and offer a small willingness to listen…without judgment…and allow for the possibility of something other than what we think to emerge. You are surely on this journey if you are reading these words. My hope is that what you find here will speak to your heart and in so doing bring you the opportunity for the emergence of your own beautiful Higher SELF.*

*Anne DiDomenico*
*February, 2009*

## THE INNER BRIDGE HOME

The door to higher consciousness
is found within the heart

here is where you access
the inner bridge home

only one thing is needed….
willingness to let go

you are here to do just this:

awaken yourself
to the treasure
you thought
was left behind and lost

Beautiful one of the light…
who you are…
what you are…
can never be lost…
only forgotten….for a time

and now….in the awakening
you are remembering

the door to your heart
opens wide
to receive the endless love
All That Is supplies

with great joy
you are received
into the arms of a loving Father

*your heart knows the truth*
*without words or fanfare*
*but rather with a simplicity*
*that enraptures your very soul*

*open the inner door*

*crossover the inner bridge*

*the arms of Love are waiting for you*

# Table of Contents

# PART ONE:
# REMOVING THE VEIL

*when we bless all that is unlike love,*

*we remove the veil*

## *THE VEIL*

*when we bless all that is unlike love,*

*we remove the veil*


*resistance is the veil*

*pride is the veil*

*violence is the veil*

*fear is the veil*


*bless all of this without judgment,*

*and remove the veil*

## *CHOOSE LOVE*

*each choice for love*
*is a choice for claiming my heritage*

*each choice for love*
*is a choice to remember who i am*

*when i choose love…*
*i choose freedom*
*and my heart has wings*

*when i choose love…*
*what appears unlike love dissolves*
*and the veil is removed*

*choice powers the journey*

*Love is the destination*

## SURRENDER

*i close my eyes
and surrender my entire being
to the Voice for Love*

*i see all that is unlike love
coming out from within me*

*placing it on a silver tray
i hand it to my beloved Self*

*who takes what i have created
in separation and innocence*

*and transforms it all into
pure love....its original state*

*clear and released
from the bondage
of disowned creations*

*i now know the Truth of all i see*

## *MOVING OUT OF DENSITY*

*moving out of density
into higher dimensional reality…*

*there is a shifting of emotional
awareness,
where sensations
are no longer felt in the body
the same way*

*experience is of a higher vibrational rate
and as a result
we know ourselves in a different way
one that is both familiar and new*

*we are moving into a state of knowing
no questions…..no doubts…...no duality…
no conflicts…...no inner turmoil….
only peace…...love…...knowing…...*

*here… separation is not known*

*the door opens to a new world
to a new way of creative existence
and we meet each other
as equals….as aspects of the One*

*here we know only love….*

*how incredible!*

*imagine knowing only love!*

*a new adventure awaits us!*

### *REMEMBER*

*i am here to remember...*
*remember my beautiful Self*
*the Self created from Source*
*the beloved Giver of Life*

*i have never left home...*
*simply forgotten in a moment*
*of desire for experience of the 'other'*

*now....i remember i am home*
*and it is truly in communion with*
*those beloved reflections i 'see'*
*that my divinity is realized.*

### *I LIVE IN MY STORY*

*I live in my story…..*

*remaining true to the plot line
of separation that i choose*

*until i awaken to the possibility
of another story*


*this other story brings me hope*

*yet i need courage and conviction*

*to move out of the old and into
the new 'remembered' story*


*separation is what i have
immersed myself in for so long*


*in comparison, the 'new' story seems
so far-fetched*

*yet…it feels soooooo good*

*when it comes as a thought
to my mind*


*i love the story of heaven
and who i am*

*i love seeing all as love coming
to me*

*and i love remembering i am here
to love all that is unlike love....*

*to remember that this is
my creation....*

*and that i call myself home*

*by remembering to love all*

## *VALUING SELF*

*it has been a long time in coming....*
*this valuing self....*
*the struggle has been with the image*
*i imagined my self to be*


*and now.......*
*as the image fades away*
*like a line drawing*
*on a water soaked page*
*i see my Self.....my true Self*
*appearing*


*the picture moves out of the invisible*
*into the visible inch by inch*
*until i see it begin to merge*
*with the self i once identified*
*only with the body*


*how beautiful is this Self i see!*
*how amazing!*
*how extraordinary!*

*and the beauty of it all is that....*
*i see it everywhere!*

## *LOVE'S PRESENCE*

*look out to the horizon's edge......*

*the endless sky speaks*


*enter here this blissful space*

*as clouds blithely glide past*

*simple…..quiet…..glorious…..*


*…..sky......clouds....*

*…….endless perfection.......*

*they all exist in a consciousness*

*that knows only peace*


*here, in this picture of serenity*

*Love breathes in and out*

*the power of presence in the Now*

## *HEART REVOLUTION*

*the mind serves the heart in all ways*
*for the heart...*
*when allowed to live its truth*
*seeks to extend itself to all*

*the heart brings Truth*
*to the experiences of our lives*
*if we but allow it*

*do we dare live*
*from the very heart of our being?*

*do we dare cross*
*the imaginary line*
*between mind and heart?*

*do we dare value*
*the heart to lead our lives?*

*what revolution would we dare*
*to conceive of*
*that would bring us to live*
*from the heart.....*
*with the mind present*
*only to serve*
*that which extends*
*the holiest within us?*

*it is time, dear ones,*
*to live from the heart.....*

*to know all as Love.....*
*to know that God dwells within all*
*and extends out from all*

*all that is needed to see this*
*is Holy Vision........*

*and this, dear ones,*
*comes from the heart*

## *WAY OF THE HEART*

*open your heart*
*to the possibility*
*of seeing your Self*
*in the 'other'*

*can you walk a mile*
*in the 'other's' shoes?*

*can you feel the*
*emotional life that exists in the 'other'*
*that also reflects your own?*

*this is the way of the heart….*

*to see your Self in all 'others'*
*to know your Self in all 'others'*
*is to know the One*

*all you see…*
*without exclusion…*
*is you, dear one*

*all life….*
*all is You*

*You are the One…*

*You are all you 'see'*

## DISSOLVE INTO LOVE

the ocean.....vast.....deep.....wide

moving into infinity....

it is the sea of love

and i am the One

as i dissolve into Love

no longer knowing the small self identity

embracing the grand Self that I AM....

the dewdrop and the ocean
one and the same

my being dissolves into

Oneness

as Truth speaks to me

## *RELEASE JUDGMENT*

*bring your willingness*
*to embrace all*


*free your self*
*from the one choice*
*you have made*
*that imprisons you....*

*that you are separate*
*from all you see.....*


*embrace all in your world*


*and in this act*
*you release your self*
*from the prison of judgment....*

*you decree freedom upon your self*

## *NOTHING TO DO*

*there is nothing to do but this:*

*bless all*

*love all*

*extend all to all*

*all else is illusion*

## *JUST FOR A MOMENT*

*breathe in.....breathe out.....*

*become the observer of your life*


*just for a moment*

*look at what is unfolding before you,*
*and know that all is occurring*
*for the highest good of all*


*just for a moment*

*observe your life*
*with no attachment to outcome...*
*with no thought of vested interests...*


*observe, as the Father observes,*
*and know without doubt*
*that all is in perfection....*


*All is Love*

### THE FIRES WITHIN*

the raging fires that appear outside
of ourselves
are the reflection of fires within
calling for the clearing waters
of love and blessings


as we embrace what comes,
the moment tempers
and calm is restored
with a peace that is eternal


the heart of love knows these times....
and welcomes them

knowing this as the moment
of transition
into a state beyond which cannot
presently be seen


(written during severe 2008
California fires)

## *BLESS IT ALL*

*the sun warms me thru and thru,*

*and I bless it*

*in a sweet moment of Life,*

*I experience joy,*

*and I bless it*

*from 'another's' reflection of myself*

*comes pain and disappointment,*

*and I bless it*

## HEALING THE PAST

the pain of past memories
rises up in me
and I feel lack….

the lack of my capacity to love
in that very moment of memory…
when love was calling out to me…..

my heart feels such pain
in this moment


and then…..

a blessed thought arises in my
Holy Mind…

to bless what has just appeared….
to bless the pain and
the belief in lack


in this way, healing occurs,

for what appears to be pain and lack
is now seen for the illusion it is,

and love comes home
to its own

## *MY NOW OF THE PAST*

*i allow the past to become
my Now….*

*to bless what comes
and give it to Love*

*in this conscious moment,*

*painful memories
transform before me,*

*as Love shows me the Truth
that love is all there is…*

*and now…..the past…..*

*made new in the light of Love….*

*dwells in the peace of my Holy Mind*

## *MERGING MIND AND HEART*

*there is a merging taking place.....*

*a joining of the seemingly separate*

*into the One Heart*

*i feel the merging*

*there is this sensation*

*that is without words.....*

*transitioning out of duality*

*as the mind and heart realize*

*Oneness*

*in all that is seen…felt…heard…*

*how extraordinary*

*to be witness....to be part of*

*this merging of self with Self*

## *THE UNDOING PROCESS*

*it is not true that
"what is done is done."
it is in choosing differently
that you allow undoing to occur*


*it is in the undoing of your creations
dear one,
that you find your way home*


*allow all that is unlike love…..
unlike peace……..unlike joy……..
to come to you for healing*


*and you do this, dear one,
by blessing each of these creations
without judgment…without opinion….
as they arise in your feeling center….*

*remembering that all of creation is
innocent…
for you are innocent.*


*in blessing all that comes to you,
you undo your mis-creations,
and in that moment of blessing,
you create anew according to your desires*

*is it peace you desire?
then choose peace consciously and ongoingly.*

*is it love you desire?*
*then this, too....choose consciously and*
*ongoingly*

*and joy.....*
*it is yours simply by choosing it*


*in this way, you undo what you*
*no longer desire*

*in this way you create a new Now*
*and draw to you more of the same*

## *HEART / MIND ALIGNMENT*

*give all to gain all….*

*dear ones…*

*give the lower self*
*to the Higher Self….in surrender*

*open to your heart speaking*

*bringing your mind into alignment*

*thus……*

*inner conflict is resolved*
*and*
*centeredness…..wholeness….*
*is manifested*

*as heart and mind speak in unison:*

*"We are One…….*

*within this entity…..*

*We are One…..*

*and all creation is in wholeness"*

# PART TWO:
# NEW CHOICES

*you experience Love*

*when   Y_O_U*

*make the decision for it*

ANNE DIDOMENICO

### FREE YOUR SELF

when you liberate your mind
from the attachment to form

you are free


you experience Love
when   **Y_O_U**
make the decision for it


Love can be experienced

by anyone

at any time

in any place

about anything


it is always............
..............and simply


a choice

## *I AM FREE TO CHOOSE*

*responsibility is freedom*

*freedom*

*to change your mind…*

*to choose*

*again….*

*to create*

*anew*

## *BRIDGE TO THE ONE*

*you walk*

*the bridge of transformation…*

*from self.………...…..…….*

*……………...to…………...*

*…………………...…..SELF*

*and as you*

*observe this movement…*

*know that you are*

*the very bridge you cross…*

*know that you are both*

*the small self and the grand SELF*

*merging*

*in recognition*

*of that which you are…*

*the One*

## *THERE IS ONLY GOD*

*when you make*

*the simple choice*

*to release resistance*

*allowing all things to flow…*

*you discover*

*that all along*

*there has only been*

*God*

### *DESIRE TO LOVE*

*within every heart*
*lies a desire to love*

*desire is of the Father…*
*the creative spark*
*that lights the way…*

*love you each and every moment*

*and know each moment*
*to be your choice…*
*your will……*

*to choose love…*

*yet, whatever your choice*
*in any moment…*

*know this:*

*your will is God's will*

*there is only one will…*

*for you are the extension*
*of the Creative Principle*

*there is no separation*
*between you and God*

*you are one with your Father*
*as you extend love…*

*all Life......all Creation.....*

*sit in this statement....*

*I and the Father are One.*

### *LIVE THE SIMPLE LIFE*

*can you imagine*

*living the simple life?*

*the first step: TRUST*

*TRUST*
*all is perfect as it is*

*TRUST*
*you will be provided for*

*TRUST*
*you live in abundance*

*the second step: KNOWING*

*KNOW*
*you ARE perfection*

*KNOW*
*you ARE the provisions you desire*

*KNOW*
*you ARE abundance itself*

*Live from your I AM Presence*

## *EMBRACE ALL*

*embrace all*

*and*

*total freedom is yours*

## FIELD OF PEACE

*Creation stands in waiting for my desire...*

*consciously choosing peace*

*activates the field of peace*

*that brings to me*

*all i have created unlike peace*

*in this way,*

*i bless my mis-creations*

*created in innocence*

*and clear the way for peace*

*to truly enter*

## *PONDER THIS......*

*healing.…..forgiveness.…..*
*are not needed*
*but for a belief in separation..….*

*surrender, trust, patience..….*
*tools used by a mind*
*still residing in duality.…..*

*once the realization comes*
*that the Atonement is complete.….*
*the mind residing in duality*
*moves to right-mindedness*
*where Knowing*
*is the state of mind.….*

*here,*

*the eyes of Christ see only Love.…..*
*know only Truth.…..*

*you are the One, dear one.…..*

*remember.….*

### *KNOW YOUR HEART*

*to your own Self be true….*

*know your heart…*

*this is where your truth lies*

*and your truth is yours uniquely*

*doubt is of the ego….the small self
and the world of illusion…*

*to enforce conformity upon yourself
is to create pain and suffering…*

*when you create alignment
of heart and mind within..…*

*you experience a gentleness
about it…
a love and caring for Self…*

*here…*

*you find your truth…
your peace…*

*you open the door to Heaven….
and all possibility*

## *RESPONSIBILITY IS FREEDOM*

*acknowledge your beliefs....*
*see how they create your reality....*

*know your innocence in all of this*
*and that now.....*

*in this moment of awareness.....*
*you have a choice*

*in this,*
*the gift of true freedom dwells*

*take responsibility for all you see.....*

*bless it.....*
*know your innocence.....*
*and choose again.....dear one.....*

*this time.....*
*choose love*

## *DISCOMFORTING THOUGHT*

*there is a feeling here....*
*unnamed......yet felt within...*
*uncomfortable as it sits in me...*

*what is it that feels so edgy.....*
*so contracted?*

*ahhhh.....competition....i see.....*
*I notice the edges of it*
*rising up*
*in me*

*my first response says 'no'*
*i want to push it away...*
*I don't like this feeling...*

*the next moment says 'allow'*

*so i take a breath*
*and allow this feeling...*

*and with it comes guilt...shame...*
*disappointment in the thought:*
*"i should know better."*

*and in the next moment*
*another thought....*

*"indeed, i do know better.*
*i know to allow it.....*
*to own it.....to bless it.*
*i DO know better."*

*this road i walk is one of peace...*
*nothing can disturb this...*

*thoughts and feelings*
*arise and fade...*

*all I need do*
*is observe....allow.....own....bless*

*and where a moment before*
*a thought of competition arose*

*now.....*
*there is only peace.....*
*and gratitude for awareness*

## *OUTSIDE IN & INSIDE OUT*

*why do you continue to live*
*a life of loss......a life of lack?*

*if you look at this, you will see*
*that your vision is coming*
*from the  o u t s i d e in...*

*do you not notice that when you*
*'see' lack anywhere*
*it is your own projection*
*of a belief in lack?*

*an entrenched belief in lack*
*makes 'seeing' lack possible*

*there is a remedy....*

### *Change your belief!*

*see the world with new eyes*

*be willing to see love's presence*
*where before you saw only lack*

*be willing to re-interpret*
*what you see*

*instead of anger and violence*
*see a cry for help*

*re-interpret pain and suffering*
*as a call*
*to awareness and new thought*

*decide now to see everything*
*differently...*

*decide now to release judgment...*

*for judgment of what you 'see'*
*and judgment of your self...*
*are one and the same thing.*

*when you come to accept this as*
*true*
*you will stop all judgment*

*when you understand that judgment*
*creates pain and suffering*
*you will release it*

*in this release, you free yourself...*
*and when you free yourself,*
*you free the world*

*now, you 'see' from*
*the i n s i d e out...*

*now, you 'see' from*
*the very heart of Love...*

*and lack in any form, dear ones,*
*becomes the very opportunity*
*to 'see' Love*

## *CALL TO HEAVEN*

*so often you call to the heavens*
*for help…*
*your cries are always heard….*
*always….*

*yet, you believe you are not heard*
*since what you think you 'want'*
*does not appear…*

*have you considered*
*that your calls are answered…*
*in the only way you will allow?*

*have you considered*
*that when the answer is different*
*than you imagined it to be…*

*it is because you are….*
*unwilling….*
*to see what is before you*
*as the answer?*

*if you do not believe*
*you are worthy of heaven on earth*
*you will not allow heaven to manifest*

*dear one…*
*your belief that life is a struggle….*
*your belief in pain and suffering*
*limit you to only those experiences*

*only YOU can change this…*
*only YOU have the power of choice*
*within your reality…*

*beloved, see with the eyes of love*
*and open to all possibilities…*

*allow…*

*release all judgment*
*and allow…*

*this is how you clear*
*the pathways of communication*
*between your heart*
*and the One Mind of heaven*

*if you do this,*
*you will see with new eyes…*

*you will see that everything*
*you have asked for*
*is sitting there before you*

*waiting for you to recognize it*
*as the answer…*

*waiting for you to allow it*
*to be the answer…*

*judgment prevented you*
*from seeing it*

*now, in allowance you see*
*with new eyes*
*and the world is new*
*as you allow it to be as it is…*

*for you and heaven*
*have joined forces*
*and now see as one*

*when you change your mind*
*about what is possible for you…*

*about who you are*
*and your worthiness…*

*your cries for help*
*become songs of gratitude*

*your world is seen*
*as only Love*
*manifesting in perfection*

*this becomes your only Reality*

## *JUDGING*

*you are God and in that*

*you are free to judge yourself*

*by judging 'another'…*

*and in doing this*

*you create your own*

*perfect experience*

*of feeling the effects of judging…*

*and then….as God….*

*you are free to love your creations*

*and choose anew*

*for a different experience*

### EYES TOWARD HEAVEN

*leave the world as it is…*
*an illusion……and only that…..*

*let nothing here compel you…*

*set your eyes to heaven*
*to the mastery of the small self*
*and the giving of your presence*
*to others*


*dear ones, you are born of Love…*
*this Love lives in you eternally…*

*it cannot die…*
*it cannot be extinguished…*
*but it can be forgotten for a time*


*when sadness and despair*
*rule your life*
*when depression sets in*
*know you have forgotten*
*the true Life that lives in you*

*tell yourself when this happens*
*you will remember…*

*and in times of challenge*
*a loving thought of reminder*
*will come to you*

*leave the world as it is,*
*dear ones,*
*let nothing compel you…*

*with eyes turned toward heaven*
*you will return home again*

**GROWING PAINS**
*for Chad*

with tears of joy
i cradled you…
my precious infant son…
cradled you in my arms….

you…..so sweet….so innocent
in every way…..

my heart filled with love
as i held you close
believing this would
protect you
from an unloving world.

yet, during your childhood years
i came to a knowing…

that only from within
could real protection come…
no 'outside' force
could alter your destiny.

you grew to manhood
and found your way…
experiencing your ups and downs
with the deepest of emotions.

and thru it all
i learned…
you had to live this life
in your own way…
with your own choices…

*it was your right.*

*i have always known this*
*although, at times,*
*fear prevented me from living it fully.*

*as you evolved…*
*so did i…*

*then…...one day….*
*i knew the time had come*
*so, with loving arms*
*and a heart filled with trust…*

*i released you*
*to your Higher Self*
*allowing you total freedom…*
*to live your life*
*as you would have it….*

*knowing full well*
*you were…and have always been…*
*in the care of the heavenly Father*

*i knew your safety was assured,*
*for now,*
*my fear had been replaced by trust.*

*you see, my darling child,*
*while you were growing up*
*i was growing up, too.*

## I SIMPLY ASK THE QUESTION

is the desert experience necessary?

is it the only way to arrive home?

must i wade thru the pain and
suffering of so many years past
in order to....once again....
rejoin the love i am?

if this is the only way
then i accept it as it is and move thru
the trial i have created for my self....

yet....somewhere in me
there is a voice

that says it can be different
if i choose....

i can be in that place
...of perfect peace...
perfect love...…………..
…………..perfect joy.....
now…......

no suffering needed.....

can i create that experience for
myself in this moment?

am i worthy……………....
…………….deserving ....
of experiencing the love that i am

*without going through*
*the trials and tribulations*
*of meeting my mis-creations?*

*i simply ask the question......*

## *DISCERNMENT*

*know you discernment?*

*when you have questions…
choices to make…*

*how do you know what is best
for you?*

*where do you go within yourself
to make those decisions?*

*dear ones,
discernment lies within the heart*

*here you will find your truth
for any question you ask or choice
you make*

*this is a moment to moment experience…
a journey taken by you alone
not to be confused or compared
with another's*

*each of you is called to find your own way
thru the heart of love that speaks to you*

*neither judgment nor criticism lives here
only love…..*

*and the particular choice
that is right for you*

*allow others their path
for their journey is uniquely their own*

*honor theirs as you honor your own*
*as perfect…*
*… for it is*

*so, my dear ones, your heart*
*is the center of discernment*

*allow it to be the director of your life*
*allow it full expression*

*it is waiting for your*
*acknowledgement*
*so it can bring you the joy*
*you deeply desire*

*your heart knows love*
*when it meets it*

*when it comes to love*
*it is on automatic pilot*

*allow it to act on your behalf*
*open to the unknown possibilities*
*yet to come*

*it is only thru the heart*
*that this can occur*

*only thru the heart will you find*
*your center for discernment*

## PAIN

when pain appears……
resistance is present
energy is blocked
and 'what is' cannot be received

dear one, I ask you…..
are you willing to 'see' with new eyes?

are you willing to allow
the un-allowable?

are you willing to accept
the un-acceptable?

are you willing to forgive
the un-forgivable?

change your mind…
see what is before you
as your creation

own it

know it comes in love to you
from YOU

it is exactly what you need
there is no mistake

this creation of yours
offers the perfect opportunity
to bring heaven to earth

*this creation of yours*
*contains all the elements needed*
*to bring you home to your true Self.*

*love it*

*love it all*

*leave no part and no one*
*outside your love*

*every element in your creation*
*contains the seeds of your rebirth*

*so the pain you feel in this moment*
*is simply re-birthing pains*

*it heralds your re-entry into*
*the Reality you never left*
*but thought you did*

*with this knowing*
*firmly planted in you now….*
*you serve your true Self*
*in highest measure.*

## *NO MISTAKES*

*there are no mistakes…..*

*you cannot make a wrong turn….*

*regret not any thought, word
or action…..*

*for in each of these moments
of choice…*

*you were God*

*choosing to have an experience*

*……..and now……*

*……...as God……*

*you choose again*

### *ONLY ONE MIND*

*all choice is made*

*within the One Mind…*

*the field of Love*

*….tears…..pain…..fear…..*
*……suffering…..*

*chosen by you for experience…*

*even these exist*

*as your creations*

*within the One Mind*

*until your time of awakening*

*when Love rather than fear*

*fuels your every choice.*

## LOVING NOTES FROM MY SELF

*you need do nothing*
*but allow that channel within*
*to be your guidance….*

*it is not your purpose to 'survive'…*
*however…..*

*it IS your purpose*
*to be the extension of Love…*

*set aside all attachments*
*to the illusions of the body-mind*

*improve your life*
*by seeing your true nature*

*decide to listen only*
*to the voice within…*

*there is nothing to seek….*

*dear one….*
*liberate your mind*
*from the 'wrongs' of the world*

*where a fearful thought arises*
*you have simply forgotten love…*

*the world of form*
*can never be*
*the world of perfect freedom*

*identify with form*
*and suffering occurs*

*how can you extend love in this moment?*

*open you heart…………..*
*………open your arms…..*

*and receive the Reality of Love*
*that is ever present for you*


**love your Self**


**the experience of love is a decision**


*celebrate the love that you are*
*and ask:*

*how can I extend Love now?*


*there is nothing else you need to do*

### *AWAKEN*

*awaken to the realization that*

**You are the power...**
*in this illusion called the physical
world...*

*where you appear as a body-mind...
where you appear to be subject to
insecurities…....aging…....death…....*

*in awakening...
you realize that
you are the power
who chooses to experience this  belief!*

*when this realization falls upon you
you are free to step out of
the dark night of the soul
and embrace your sovereignty*

*you are free
to become your own authority
to listen only to the voice within*

## *LIVE FROM THE HEART*

*when you make the choice*

*to say yes to Love…*

*to live from your heart…*

*you allow the space for possibility*

*dear ones,*

*make every choice*

*a conscious choice for Love…*

*in this way,*

*you create your heart's*

*deepest desire*

# PART THREE:
# INNER SPACE

*Silence*

*is the doorway*

*to deep honesty with self*

ANNE DIDOMENICO

## SILENCE #1

*the Kingdom within lives*

*in the silence of my Holy Mind*

*silence is that space that invites*

*the Voice for Love to speak*

*to my heart*


**Silence**

**is the doorway**

**to deep honesty with self**

## *SILENCE #2*

*in the silence,*

*i listen for the Voice for Love*

*in the silence, my heart speaks*

*and my Holy Mind listens*

*for it knows its own…*

*it knows the voice of Truth.*

*in the silence,*

*i meet my Self and am whole…*

*in absolute peace with all of creation*

## THIS MOMENT

*loving arms embrace me*

*with such warmth*

*there can be no mistaking*

*the love that envelops me*

*as I sit quietly with Self*

*in this moment*


*how sweet…*

*how beautiful…*

*to experience tenderness...*

*complete acceptance...*

*allowing peace to arise as experience*

*within this body now*

ANNE DIDOMENICO

## THE SEA OF NOT KNOWING #1

the sea of not knowing…
where I do not know
what anything is or is for
emerges for me
as a new way of being…

where flow replaces agenda

where time is not even a thought

the living of life
is transformed within me,
and can only be described
as living/being
in the absolute NOW

## THE SEA OF NOT KNOWING #2

the sea of not knowing…bewildering
at first…
as I seek to be oriented
in the grayness of my mind…

the usual markers (beliefs) are gone,
as the thought comes that
i know not what anything is or is for

"How shall I proceed," I ask my Self


"Wait….be still
Breathe into the moment,
and you will know, beloved, without
doubt

You will feel it in your heart center,
and the knowing
of action or non-action
will be self-evident…
without question"


the sea of not knowing
ushers me into a new reality
where only Love exists

and as I hold this single thought:
only Love exists,

acceptance and allowance
naturally extend from me
in each moment….

*the eternal NOW....*
*the only moment*

*and blessing all*
*becomes*
*my only purpose*

### *REFLECTING*

*time passes....*
*changes occur....*

*the human form… just like the leaf*
*experiences the effects of belief.…*

*for the leaf is solely a projection*
*of what you believe to be true....*

*you live…..you die….*
*is this not a belief?*

*is this not what is reflected in nature*
*as you….the creator..…*
*made it to be?*

*and now....*
*allow a new belief to stir within you...*
*a belief that all exists*
*eternally beautiful and unchanging*

*where the leaf remains*
*lovely and supple...*
*brilliant with true color...*
*alive to the truth of its source.…*

*allow it now to reflect*
*the knowing of eternal life*
*that you are*

## *SOLITUDE*

*there is sanctuary in solitude…*

*the Self,*

*my constant companion*

*here,*

*the Voice for Love speaks to me*

*Truth is present in every breath…*

*in every thought*

*gratitude to All That Is*

*for Life Itself*

## TRUE AND HOLY SELFISHNESS

to 'acquire' for yourself is a God-given instinct....
and the learning is this:

to get is to give.....

true giving benefits all, and in this
you benefit your Self......
the only Self there is

To heal yourself of illness....
send healing thoughts
to those who are ill

To bring love into your life.....
send loving thoughts
to all without exception

To know true peace of mind......
send peace-filled thoughts
in every moment

Willingly give
from your heart/ mind aligned......
and all will come to you

True and holy selfishness:

give all to receive all

## *KNOW ONLY LOVE*

*be not of this world....*

*but instead*
*be as the child*
*in a field of beauty*
*moving with the wind....*
*soaring with the birds......*

*be not of this world....*

*but instead*
*know thy innocence....*
*the simplicity of joy in every moment*
*delighting in the creativity*
*that extends from a mind*
*that knows only Love*

## SWEET PEACE

….the sun warms me….

….the breeze caresses me….

…...the ocean sounds fill me…....

sweet peace….

in this moment…….sweet peace

ANNE DIDOMENICO

## EACH STEP SACRED

*focus in this moment…*
*hold awareness of each step you take*

*for as you place your feet*
*upon the earth…*
*you touch sacred ground*

*each step…….sacred*
*for you, my beloved, are sacred…*

*the manifested Christ*
*walking upon sacred energy*
*appearing as solid matter.*

*beloved child of the Father,*
*if you would but focus*
*in this moment…*

*allow awareness to show you*
*the very Love that you are…*

*see this Love rising up within you…*
*as you walk the planet*
*manifesting the consciousness*
*of the one Christ*

*gently…*
*mindfully…*
*live the sacredness*
*of each step you take*

## *SIT IN SILENCE*

*sit by flowing water…*
*contemplate inner knowing…*

*a drop of water in the stream*
*knows not judgment of its self*
*nor does it know judgment*
*of other drops of water*
*in the stream…*

*it simply flows*
*with the energy of the stream*

*can you be as the drop of water?*

*can you manifest the love*
*that you are*
*and flow with the stream of life?*

*allow this realization to*
*come forward…*

*you are loved*
*you are that love*
*you are in the flow of that love*

*you are the journey*
*of the stream itself*

## *BE*

*to be*

*in the perfection of the moment*


*to be with all*

*yet....*

*with no thought*

*other than to be present*

*as the observer...*


*no thought.................................*
*...........no sound............*
*.................................no movement*


*the observer....*

*simply being love's presence*

*in utter simplicity*

## *SWEET GRATITUDE*

*the sweetness of gratitude*
*pours into my being....*

*a universal pitcher of endless love*
*finds its way 'into' me......*
*...........and 'out' through me*
*as easily as a glass*
*fills with water and i drink it down*

*easy.......yes.......*

*ordinary.........no......*

*gratitude is the radiant*
*flow of a loving universe....*

*unstoppable in the light manifested*

*endless in the joy expressed*

*brilliant in the feeling experienced*

*the sweetness of gratitude*
*has no equal......*

## *EVERY BREATH*

*with every breath*
*i turn my thoughts to love....*

*this is my choice*
*now and forever....*

*to KNOW the love i am*
*to extend that which i am to all*

*with every breath*
*i live in you, my beloved,*

*and together we create*
*the good, the holy, and the beautiful*

*choose love and we co-create*
*the beauty that we are as*
*all unlike love falls away*

*as the only Reality....LOVE*
*is embraced within you....*
*as the creator*

*all is given life thru me*
*from the Source*

*all is Love*

### HOW TO LOVE SELF

Beloved Child of the Light,
know you how to love your Self?

it is an in-side job

breathe into each moment

and…f_ e_ e_ e_ e_ l…the heart.

what does it tell you?

what words does it speak to you?

live your passion ….
live your heart's desire….

in this way, you love the Self
who experiences life through you

**it is not the outward 'things' that
bring you love
but it is you, dear one,
who brings love to each experience**

in doing this,
you experience Self-love….

you experience the love
that you are….

…Love rising up in you
projecting Itself outward

*so that it manifests into physical form*
*to be experienced in a new way*


*Self-love occurs*
*when you create from the heart*
*recognize your creation*
*and love it*

*such awareness of this allows you*
*to experience your Self*
*…the true Self…*
*in every moment*

## *THE UN-REAL CYCLE*

*resistance is fear*

*fear is illusion*

*illusion is separation*

*separation is un-real*


*your job:*

*un-do the un-real*

## *STEP BACK*

*when you step back*
*and observe your life*

*in the small amount of time*
*it takes for one breath,*

*you allow the Self*
*to bring you what you need*

*in that brief moment of breath,*
*knowing is present…*
*answers come…*
*for action or non-action*

*in that conscious moment of breath,*
*you allow your KNOWING*
*to rise to your conscious mind*

*you allow space*
*for Divine Intervention*
*to enter your life*

## *UNCONDITIONAL LOVE*

*love allows all…….*

*…..….embraces all*

*……so..…*

*even that which would appear*

*to be unlike love*

*exists*

*in the arms*

*of Unconditional Love*

## *TRUE KNOWLEDGE*

*true knowledge ......*

*what is it?*

*FULL PRESENCE*

*in this moment....*

*observing all that arises*

*in perfect innocence*

*here lies your peace*

*here lies right-mindedness*

## DESIRE FOR LOVE

*it is my desire for love*
*that brings love to me*

*the words.....the people....*
*the places.....*
*the very energy of love*

*calls me out of my self*
*that i may see my Self*

*i am cause and effect*

*i am the thought…………..*
*………..…….the thinker*
*and the result…….*

*i am the writer………..……....*
*…………..…producer*
*director….……*
*…………………….and actor*

*to know this at the core of my being*
*is to come home*

*there is only the One*

*All is One*

## *LOVE ONE ANOTHER*

*Beloved child of the Father…*
*do you remember these words:*
*love one another?*

*see in another*
*the face of Christ…*

*see in another*
*your very divinity*

*know your Self to be Love…*

*and as you take this in…*
*as you look into another's eyes…*
*know them to be Love as well*

*make no distinctions….no judgments*

*be committed, dear one,*
*to seeing only Love*
*in all that passes before you*

*once you are out of time*
*you will know the Truth*
*and be grateful for your commitment*
*while on the planet…*

*to see only Love…..be only Love….*

### *YOUR HERITAGE*

*you are already perfect
did you know that?*

*beloved, you are perfection itself
you cannot be other than perfection
in the Truth of your I AM-ness*

*can you accept your identity
as one with the Source of All?*

*can you make the choice
to accept this as true?*

*how long before you realize
that it is the voice of self-doubt alone
that prevents your awakening?*

*how long before you say:
no more lies to myself about
who I am….
no more self-deception, distractions
or lack of focus*

*allow the commitment of your heart
to speak:*

**i am ready
i am ready now to claim
my true heritage
I am one with my heavenly Father
I am one with that Creative Source**

**it is thru me that the Source extends
and expresses.**

*I claim this heritage,*
*and allow this loving Creative Power*
*to move in me......thru me......*
*with me*

*I am Joy*

*I am Love*

*I am Christ awakened*

## *HEART VALUE*

*the contents of the heart is all
that can be given…
it is the only thing
of real value…*

*all giving from the heart
is always a gift of love*

*giving without the heart….
out of some misconstrued idea
of obligation or duty
is bereft of meaning…a mis-creation*

*value what is eternal
and unending…
and that, dear one,*

*…is simply…
….solely…*

*…Love…*

*the one gift of the heart
residing in all
without exception*

*yet, 'appearing' in those alone
who have made the choice
to give only Love*

## *EACH DAY*

*each day…*
*as you awake…*

*remember to ask:*

*what would Love have me do today?*

*and then…..*
*allow the Silence*
*to speak to you*

*in this way….*
*you allow the I AM Presence*
*to extend Itself…*

*in this way….*
*you remember your purpose*

## NOW

*i see that i am being gently
and sometimes
not so gently nudged
to live in the NOW….*

*nudged to free my mind
of past and future….
of worries and concerns
that cloud my vision*

*the call within is to surrender all…
value nothing but Love
in the moment…*

*to yield to the Voice For Love
who would have me sing and rejoice
in each waking/sleeping moment*

*it speaks to me in gentle tones…*

*"Yield, blessed one, to the flow
of life within you…
feel into that loving vortex
of energy that knows not time
or space*

*expand into forever-ness
and lose all thought
for other than NOW*

*here, and only here,
lies your true Reality
your true identity…
your true home…*

*b r e a t h e into the N O W*

*b r e a t h e with Me....*

*.....and together*

*we b r e a t h e into f o r e v e r...*

*Peace.....joy.....love....*

*it is all yours...*

*N O W"*

### SOUL/SOLE PURPOSE

*know that your soul/sole purpose*
*is to extend your very nature*
*which is Love*

*you do this by*

### K_N_O_W_I_N_G

*every moment as perfect*
*and as the opportunity*
*to extend Love*

### LISTEN

*only to the voice within you*

### KNOW

*there is nothing to seek…*
*there are no mistakes…*

### ALL IS PERFECT AS IS

*your choices,*
*when made from the heart of Love,*
*serve always the whole of creation*

### ask yourself:

### how can I extend Love
### in this moment?

*in this way*
*you serve your Self*
*and all Life*

*seemingly separate, yet*
*in Reality....*
*one and the same*

*in this way*
*you live your only purpose*

### *RETURN HOME*

*you emerge from
the very Source of your being*

*pure Love manifesting into form….*

*you are the extension
of the Source…*

*Love extending Love in the world
of form*

*you, as pure Love,
can do nothing else but extend love*

*you are the heart and soul
of the Creator
creating as your Father creates*

*it is time now, beloved,
to be aware of this truth*

*hear the call to return home
and know only your true Reality…*

## *LOVE*

*in this way, you lift yourself…*
*and all life…*


*to know yourself as the One*
*brings all life into Oneness with you*


*with the guidance of the Holy Spirit*
*who speaks thru the heart*

*you find your way home to Love*

## *THE PATH*

*with gentle authority*
*step on to the path*
*the Father has set before you*


*your authority arises*
*from your knowing with certainty*
*who walks beside you*


*relieved of all worldly thought*
*you now live freely*
*into the choice you have made…*


*to serve the one desire*
*that lives in your Holy Mind:*


*to manifest fully and extend wholly*
*the Father's one creation…..*
*Christ, I AM*

## *THRU YOUR HEART*

*allow your heart to open and*
*give yourself to Spirit*
*so you may*
*access the innocence and purity*
*that resides within you*

*it is there...*
*it has never left you...*
*only hidden from your eyes*
*by acquired sophistications*

*you are the hope of your self*

*the choice you make*
*to open your heart*
*is your own salvation*

*this choice opens the door*
*that leads to the bridge home*

*it is only thru your heart*
*that your greatest desire is reached*
*only thru your willingness*
*to see the truth of who you are*
*is heaven realized within you*

*the heart, dear one,*
*is the doorway...*

*open your heart to me*
*allow the light of Love*
*to fill this space*
*and every avenue radiating from it*

# PART FOUR:
# WHO I AM

*Joy is my nature...*

*the point from which I create*

*all that I see*

ANNE DIDOMENICO

### *JOY IS WHO I AM*

*Joy is the very air I breathe*

*it moves in and out of me*
*singing the music of life…..of love*

*Joy fills my being*

*it dances into every cell of this body*
*powered by the I AM…*
*a joy-filled being of light*

*Joy is my nature….*

*the point from which I create*
*all that I see*

*Joyously I sing the song of love*

*Joyously I embrace each moment*
*as it unfolds before me*

*Joyously I experience myself*
*in each moment without judgment*

*blest am I to have this focus……*
*this thought for how to see…..*
*this thought for who I am.*

*a song of gratitude do I sing this day*

*this voice rises up with arms*
*outstretched*
*to receive the Love of All That Is*

*it fills my being…..*
*and I breathe in…...*

*smiles…...laughter……joy……*

*Love extends out to all from I AM*

## *MY PRESENCE*

*i love the presence that I am*

*i love the joy that bubbles up in me…*
*those moments when i know no time*
*but only timeless space*

*i love the presence that I am*

*the one who embraces the moment*
*and says, "Let's have a party.*
*Let's enjoy this wonderful moment*
*of bliss."*

*this beautiful presence…..*
*always here whenever i look….*

*whenever my attention turns to that One*
*who loves me without question…*

*this beautiful presence is here...*

*it is who I am*

## *LOVE SELF – THE WAY HOME*

*it is your mindset, dear one,*
*that holds you back*

*there is nothing in your life*
*that can do that*
*only that which you hold*
*in your mind as truth*
*stifles the very heart of you*

*your inability to move*
*in any direction*
*is proof enough that the blockade*
*stands **within** you*

*take heed of this*

*pay attention*

*what you need to change*
*is visible if you look*

*do you truly love your Self?*

*do you understand*
*what that means?*

*to love your Self is to love God*
*Self and God are one and the same*

*so I say to you: love your Self*

*and in loving your Self*
*you will find your way home*

*beloved, knowing Truth*
*is a simple step once you realize*
*that step is within you to take*

*it is a choice*

**"I choose to love my Self this day....**
**to honor my Self....**
**to be honest in all things with Self."**

*this is the way home, beloved,*
*and I wait with open arms*
*to embrace you*

## *MYSTERY OF SELF*

*i am the very mystery i explore*

*i experience the very heart of my Self*
*in all that is before me*

*in reaching out to another*
*i touch my Self*

*in taking in the beauty*
*that surrounds me*
*i embrace my Self*

*the un-foldment of life*
*is the very un-foldment of my Self...*
*in experience with Self*

*Grace is the path i walk*
*as i bless the Self i meet*
*in everyone and everything*

*the small self surrenders*
*unconditionally*
*to Grace.....to Love......*
*to All That Is*

### *POINT OF LIGHT*

*I am a point of light*

*shining in the heavens….*


*an anchor on the earth*

*holding the connection for all life…*

*holding the connection*

*for my own transformation…*


*the transfiguration called*

*Ascension*

## *IN THIS MOMENT*

*in this moment…*

*I am the peace of Heaven…*

*Love radiates from this being…*

*for I am*

*the Christ Child of the Father*

## *DAY BREAKS*

*day breaks upon a quiet ocean…*
*the moon still visible*
*in a deep blue velvet sky*

*even in its quiet,*
*the ocean speaks of power…*

*God's power…my power…*
*one and the same…*

*and the sky speaks of eternal beauty*
*as the colors transform before*
*my eyes.*

*i am all of it…*

*the ocean… the sky… the power…*
*the beauty…*

*and the colors of this being-in-form*
*that I am*

*transform before my eyes*

*as I proclaim,*

*"I am the One"*

## *NO OTHER BUT ME*

*it is all the same, i see...*
*it is all Me....always Me....*


*it is only Me i interact with*
*in every moment*

*how can that be...*
*this thought of only Me?*


*my sweet one, you are the One*
*you are the Christ*


*there is no other but you,*

*for even the Voice you hear is you*
*coming from that eternal holy space*
*you have never left.*


*Oneness, beloved,*

*all is you in Oneness*

### THE GOD OF ANNE

*The god of anne sits by the water....*

*recognizing her Self in the beauty
around.....*

*blessed be this glorious day
of awareness*

*where i sit with the I AM
of my being...*

*b r e a t h i n g  in Love*

*as yet un-manifested......*

*b r e a t h i n g  out Love*

*in manifested radiance.....*

*as glorious Thought fills this*

*out-breath...*

*...a sigh..............................*

*...........an exhalation.............*

*..........................a release........*

115

*.......of all that is unlike love......*

*......so that Love.....*

*......the only Reality......*

*......be the Truth of me.......*

### *YOUR PURPOSE*

*be in the flow of Divine Law…..*
*living fully into the Divine Purpose*
*for which you came*


*remember, dear ones,*
*you are the Christ incarnate*


*know not death of body*
*but eternal life as your Reality*

*for…*

*to manifest Christ Consciousness…*


*thru this body………….*

*…………in this moment*


*is your Divine soul/sole Purpose*

## *TOGETHER WE ARE ONE*

*together…..*
*we are the living 'parts' of our Self*

*there is only the one Self…..*
*and as we interact*
*with each other*
*we support or resist our Self….*

*as we work together…..*
*we give expression*
*to the one Self that we are…..*

*there is only the One*
*and we are that*
*as we speak the statement…..*

*"I Am the One"*

## *I AM THE SEED*

*I am the seed*

*birthed by the Father*

*in that blessed moment*

*of Creative Thought*

*I am the flower*

*forever blooming*

*into the creativity*

*of the Now*

## *TRUTH IN VISIBLE FORM*

*see your physical body as clay
in the hands of a master potter....*

*your Self refining your self
until it shines
in the radiance of Truth....*

*you are being re-created
in this blessed N O W moment....*

*bringing forward
in greater and greater visible form*

*the Love that you are
the Love you extend*

*that all may see
the Truth that is Christ*

*beloved one of the shared heart
know this to be true
in every cell of your being...*

*and in so doing.....
you present a profound declaration
of true identity
while in a world of illusion*

## OUTSIDE MY WINDOW

*outside my window…*
*the sand…blowing across the beach…*
*the rain…meeting the ocean waves…*

*and I hear a thought…*

*"This is me.….my creation.….*
*a reflection of me in this moment."*

*so, what is going on within*
*to bring such a scene to the surface?*

*there is great activity occurring.…...*
*a churning up of the old.….*

*yes, I've been here many times…*
*in the storm of inner turmoil*
*that comes before the*
*calm can appear*

*and I hear a thought…*

*"I create the storm.….*
*I create the calm.….*

*I am the storm.….*
*I am the calm…*

*I am all of it.….*

*the outside….*

*the inside…..*

*I am all of it"*

*for, in Truth,*

*I AM*

## *HOLY VISION*

*in that place of Holy Vision*

*…you are the beholder…*

*…without judgment…*

*…without opinion…*

*…looking…*

*…watching…*

*waiting on guidance for direction*

## *YOUR DIVINITY*

*You know these words as familiar:*

*Love the Lord thy God*

*with your whole heart, whole soul,
whole mind*

*and now….*

*know these words just as well:*

*remember your divinity…*

*you are Love*

## GENEROUS HEART
### for Les

dear one,
know your Self to be
the generous heart….

know that you are Love
in each act
you extend to another…

the heart that is allowed
to be open and free
knows only joy….

for it knows Itself
in the Love it extends….

to all…..
in every place…..
in every situation…..

Love is known
in the generous heart…

and you, beloved,
are that Love

## *THE BEAUTY OF ONENESS*

*dear one,*
*how greatly loved you are*

*know this*
*without doubt*

*for you are*
*the beloved of the Father*

*there is no other*

*only you, dear one,*

*and this truth*
*is to be lived....*

*live it*
*from the deepest part of your*
*being...*

*trust it without question*

*and know the truth....*

*know that you are God...*

*know that you are Love.*

### *EYES OF CHRIST*

*You are the eyes of Christ…*

*as you view what is before you
and see only love*

*You are the eyes of Christ…*

*as you meet others on the walk
and remember only love*

*You are the eyes of Christ…*

*when no thought but love
lives in your being*

*then….*

*You are the eyes of Christ*

*living the only Reality there is*

## *WHO AM I TRULY?*

*who am I truly?*

*I am the One*
*who creates music among the stars*


*who am I truly?*

*I am the One*
*who fuels explosive fireworks and*
*extends love*
*into unlimited expansion*


*who am I truly?*

*I am the One*
*who expresses boundless joy*
*and embraces all of creation*
*with great delight*


*how amazingly wonderful to be*
*the mind-boggling*
*Truth of Me!*

## *THE GOD-SINGER*

*each moment of this life*
*you sing the song of God*

*did you know you were a singer?*

*yes, dear one,*
*there have been times*
*when you sang the most beautiful*
*melodies and you were not*
*even aware….*

*at those times*
*you brought comfort*
*and a smile to another….*
*you did not know you were singing*
*My song….*

*at other times…..*
*you experienced pain*
*and suffering with another….*
*even then…..you were singing but this time*
*in a minor key….*

*you are always singing a melody*
*within the song called Love*
*and now…..with growing awareness….*
*the song rings out*
*louder….clearer....stronger....*

*the crystalline beauty of every note*
*can be heard across all of creation…*

*you, beloved one,*
*are the God-singer*

*one who brings the message*
*of Love to all who would hear....*
*to all who would open their hearts*
*to the possibility of joy experienced.*

*remember...*

*each day....each moment...*

*you are the God-singer*
*bringing the message of Love*
*to a world longing to hear...*

## *THE EXTENSION*

*your will is God's will*

*your choice is God's choice*

**listen carefully.......**

**you and God are One**

**you are the extension**
**of the One who created you**

*just like the hydraulic arm*
*of the largest machinery...*
*you are always connected*
*to the source of your power*

*the body-mind form that you inhabit*
*is God's hydraulic arm in the world...*

*each movement....each choice*
*brings an experience.....*

*God experiencing God*

## *MY SISTER AND I*
### *for Marguerite*

*i am my sister's keeper*
*for i am my sister…*

*in living this, i demonstrate*
*the truth of who i am…*

*the ultimate mastery is*
*to know the Oneness of all life…*
*to live with no trace of resistance*
*in embracing all…*

*the illusion of separation*
*is immediately known for what it is…*
*illusion*

*and its transformation from illusion to love*
*occurs simultaneously in this*
*knowing*

*i live within the kingdom of Love…*
*within the One Mind…*

*knowing Oneness as the only Reality…*
*seeing all… thru the eyes of love…*

*my sister's beauty radiates out*
*showing me my own radiance…*

*and i know…*
*she and i are one…*
*she is the reflection*
*of the very Self i love*

## *LOVE CIRCLE*

*with outstretched arms…*

*send love to a loving universe…*

*receive love from a loving universe…*

*know you are love existing within*

*a loving universe…*

### *KNOW*

### *YOU ARE*

### *THE LOVING UNIVERSE*

### *ITSELF*

## *YOUR GENIUS IS JOY*

*Beloved Child of the Father
you walk in the light of your being
always and forever of the heart*

*know who you are
and speak the words that arise
in you*

*see the wisdom residing within
waiting to be let out....*

*speak what comes in the moment
trust yourself completely*

*the cleansing waters of love
wash the windows of your soul...*

*allow them to sparkle bright
with the joy you are*

*it is in living joy
that your genius resides....*

*trust it.....*

*trust your Self
to create opportunities
to manifest it....*

*trust your Self
to extend joy in all directions
like a giant sparkler
exploding in the sky*

*live…..*

*…….breathe…...*

*…love…...……..know…*

*embrace…………...……...……..*

*…………bless………...·*

*……………………...…..allow…*

## *THE TWO ARE ONE*

*Jeshua and Self
have come to be
one energy for me*

*there is no longer a distinction*

*the two are one
as the only Reality…Love*

*to speak with Self
to receive guidance from Self
is to be in communion
with Jeshua energies*

*the connection is set
the link assured*

*in this…..
my absolute trust resides*

## *ALWAYS IT IS YOU*

*love all that you see*

*for it is*

*always and only*

*you*

*that you encounter*

## *YOU ARE GOD*

*where God is realized….*

*suffering cannot exist*

*but….*

*if God chooses….*

*suffering can be experienced*

*just remember…..*

**You are God**

## THE UN-DOER

*you are the Christ*
*in every moment*

*dissolving the illusion...*

*bringing Love to the one before you*

*you see this beloved one*
*and know your Self...*

*now...*
*see the Father's Love*
*reflecting back to you from this one*

*you are the Christ*
*dissolving the illusion called fear...*

*you, dear one,*
*are the un-doer of the world*

## LOVER OF ALL LIFE
### for Glenda

you dream a dream of life
and here you are…
appearing as the morning sun…
directing the warmth of your love
to a beloved creation called earth

your dream emerges….
in the majesty of mountains….
the vastness of oceans….
the spaciousness of deserts….
the joining of all souls….

you bring forth
an amazing dream of creation
for the soul purpose
to extend Love…

you dream the dream
of heaven upon earth
and it is so….
for….
you are the dreamer
you are the creator
you are the Lover of all Life

how very sweet this knowing is

# PART FIVE:
# COMING HOME

*to come home...*
*...desire only God*

*all you can lose...*
*is the fear of losing...*

ANNE DIDOMENICO

## COME HOME

*to come home…*
*…desire only God*

*all you can lose…*
*is the fear of losing…..*

*dear one,*
*there is nothing outside of God…*

*leave all thoughts of the world*
*behind…..*

*remove your cloak of personality…..*

*shed the skin of knowledge….*

*and enter the Void*
*where wisdom resides…..*

*God is All*

*to know God*
*desire only God…*

*be willing to pass the test of*
*nothingness….*

*are you content*
*to be nothing and know nothing*
*while in this world of duality?*

*in this choice…*
*you release all to all…..*

*in this choice…*
*you come home to God…..*

*desire only God*
*and come Home*

## *THE DREAM DISSOLVED*

*this dream i live is dissolving
into nothingness…
the dissolution of worlds imagined
for play…..to experience……
and then move on….*

*Somehow, in the dream
i forgot to remember
i was playing a game…
i forgot to remember my true identity
and in the forgetting
darkness fell upon me*

*as i cried out in the darkness,
a voice i heard….
strangely calming…….yet…
confusing in the illusion
i thought to be real…*

*"Beloved, come home…..
remember who you are
and come home."*

*Who am I?*

*the burning question within me
from ancient times
now rises to the answer….
thru the mist of confusion
i hear the words….*

*"I am God
I am the creator of all I see
I am one with All That Is*

*I and the Father are One"*

*all worlds imagined now dissolve*
*back into nothingness*
*as I reclaim my heritage…*
*and bless all of creation*

*the dream is done*

*I am the One*

### THE ONLY REALITY

*Love is real*
*it is the only reality*

*what is real cannot be threatened*
*and*
*Love Eternal is who you are*

*release limiting thoughts*
*that separate you from all others*
*release all judgment*

### NOW is the time

*reawaken to the truth that*
*you are all One,*
*and*
**Love is the only reality there is**

*embrace Love as who you are*

*know the truth of Love*
*in every cell of your body*

*live Love in your heart…*

*for, it is thru knowing Love in your heart*
*that a new world is born*

## *TRUE ABUNDANCE*

*True abundance…*
*a full heart overflowing*
*in endless giving*
*for there is nothing else to do*


*There is nothing to own*
*nothing to possess*
*there is only LOVE*


*that appears as unlimited flow of energy*
*waves of peace…of joy…*
*of perfect Knowing…*


*Love can only be allowed*
*as the breeze blowing thru the hair*
*as the snow falling gently on the trees*


*To live in a full heart*
*where only Love is the knowing*
*is to experience*
*true abundance beyond measure*

## BE AS THE OCEAN

be as the ocean

for all who choose to step into

the vastness of the new reality you live…


allow all to enter this 'your' space

where gracious peace

is the reality offered


and Oneness…

the only knowing

## *BLESS ALL*

*bless what is leaving......*

*bless what is coming.......*

*know only Oneness in all of it*

*for*

*in Truth*

*that is all there is…*

## *HEAVEN OR...*

*what an amazing thought....*

*go frolic and play.....
sing and dance....*

*how extraordinary that i can do this*

*in the midst of what appears
to be chaos*

*fear....pain....suffering*

*now appear as signs of heaven*

*unfolding before me*

*777 appears in an article*

*for wall street today*

*and the thought comes.....*

*ahhhhhh......we are moving up
from 666!*

*finally!!  great!!*

*yes, it is amazing to think of playing*

*during such times as these*


*i choose heaven*


*today…*


*it is only a thought away*

## *CENTER OF MY HEART*

*i live in the center of my heart*

*knowing all is well…*

*all is taken care of…*

*there is nothing to do*

*but to bless all*

*embrace all*

*love all*

*light surrounds the world i see*

*and i am one with peace*

*in the center*

*of my heart*

## *ABUNDANCE*

*i live in the loving hands of abundance*
*surrounded by all*
*that is good, holy and beautiful*

*the Voice within*
*sings a song of endless gratitude*
*for this now moment*

*the good, the holy and the beautiful*
*come to me*
*and with open arms i receive it all…*

*blessing it and extending it out from me*
*in every direction*

*to receive all, give all without end*

*to give all, receive all without end*

*inhale gratitude*

*exhale appreciation*

*this is your breath of life*

*embrace all*
*bless all*
*extend all*

*I AM*
*the good, the holy and the beautiful*

## *SEEK NO MORE*

*seek and find*
*the heart of understanding*
*within your being…*

*to know God…...be God-like*

*you live in the hands of the Father*
*all resources are open to you*

*see how you limit yourself*
*with thoughts of lack*

*where is your joy?*

**evoke thoughts of joy**
**within your mind**

**and…f_ e_ e_ l…the dance of joy**
**rise up in the body**

*these thoughts…...these feelings*
*bring you home to your truth*

*see the endless beauty*
*that surrounds you*

*with such eyes*
*there is only abundance*
*to be experienced in the NOW*

*rest your mind*
*in the abundance of NOW*

*can you do this, dear one?*

*for this focus on joy and abundance*
*is the way home*

*here is where you find God*
*and seeking is no more*

## *ALL GOD*

*"union" implies two  coming together….*
*"oneness" sees no other…*
*and knows only Self…*

*look out and see God*

*whatever comes into view is God…*

*the person speaking is God*
*the food eaten with delight is God*
*a moment of pain…..*
*a moment of joy…..*
*this chair to sit on…..*
*this bed to sleep in…..*

*ALL GOD*

*God is…... All That Is*
*All That Is…… is God*

*there cannot be an*
*'outside' of God….*
*nor a 'separation' from God*

*Oneness is the only Reality*

*it is the fullness of Reality….*
*encompassing unendingly…*

*i meet, eat and breathe only God*
*i am that which i meet, eat*
*and breathe*

*Oneness is the only Reality*

*…..I AM….*

*….Oneness in expression….*

## *LOVE IS TRUTH*

*it is from the heart*

*that the eyes of Christ look out*

*sights, sounds and feelings*

*know only love here.....*

*an open heart embraces the Now*

*extending the Father's Love....*

*in this space.....Love is Truth*

## *ALL I SEE IS LOVE*

*love is present
in all i see*

*my world is one
where love expresses itself
in people, spaces and things*

*all.....expressions
of the One called Love*

*all.....expressions
emanating from the One Mind*

**JOURNEY WITHIN**

*there is nothing outside of you*

*when you go within,*
*what do you find?*

*if there is only peace….*
*joy….love….compassion….*
*residing within you…*

*then this is the only lesson*
*you can teach…*

*it is the only reality*
*you can manifest…*

*and…*
*it is the only reality*
*you will experience.*

*there is nothing outside of you*

*seek first the Kingdom of God…*
*for*
**it is within you…**

*it is where you will find*
*the ultimate authority…*

*in doing this…*
*you will find that all you seek…*

*all questions…..all answers…..*
*all thoughts….all experiences….*
*all that is….lie within….*

*there is nothing outside of you…*

*for you…*
*beloved child of the Father…*

*…you are the One*
*who creates it all…*

*there is nothing outside of you*

## *AWAKENING*

*beautiful one of the light…*

*you who create*
*the world you see*

*behold the beauty*
*of the rising sun*

*as faint colors appear*
*on the horizon*

*as brightness begins*
*to light the sky*

*see in this awakening of the day*
*your own awakening*

*born and fueled*
*by your unending desire*

*to return home*
*to the Love you are*

*in this moment*
*the yet unimagined*
*speaks to you of your brilliance*

*you who outshine the sun*
*a thousand fold*

*awaken to your potential*
*awaken to your heritage*

ANNE DIDOMENICO

*you are the very image*
*you behold*

*the extraordinary beauty is you*
*the delicate shades of color are you*
*the vast stretch of horizon is you*

*imagine this…..*

*you are beholding YOU*

*and awaken now*

## *GRACE*

*Grace is…..*

*a magical transformation
occurring within
the human being*

*Grace allows for
total integration of Self
into the physical body-mind*

*bringing the experience
of God realization
into the dense-ness
of this dimension*

*Grace is the magic
that transforms
the small-self experience
to the God-Self expression
that you are*

*Grace is…..*

*magic
transformation
integration
full realization
total presence*

## *HEAVEN*

*what is Heaven?*

*it is..................................*

*this...............*

*...NOW...*
*…..................moment...*

*embraced*

*and*

*allowed*

*in love.......................*

*................unconditionally*

## DIVINE SELFISHNESS

*live in divine selfishness…*
*know you what that is?*

*dancing perfectly with your brothers*
*and sisters without judgment*
*no matter what their choice*
*no matter how they respond to you*

*live in divine selfishness…*
*and know the impossibility*
*of separation one from another…*
*the impossibility of causing another*
*to suffer*

*how can that be in the face of*
*atrocities and abuse….*
*neglect and rejection you ask?*

*"an eye for an eye…" is the belief*
*that you are separate from your brother*

*this is not true.*

*you and you brother are one*

*and when a choice appears in your*
*reality as abuse know this to be*
*a reflection of the belief in abuse*
*you carry within your own heart*

*do you have the courage to see this?*
*do you have the willingness to accept this as possible?*

167

*your brother is but your reflection*

*forgive yourself*
*by forgiving your brother…*
*forgiveness cannot happen otherwise*

*love yourself by loving your brother…*
*you cannot receive love if you hold*
*conditions for extending it*

*this is living in divine selfishness*
*when you own all and embrace all*
*as your creation*

*celebrate the Eternal Reality*
*you are*

*live in divine selfishness*
*and love all*

### *DIVINE LOVE*

*all energy is Divine Love…*
*the very expansion of the*
*radiant Self…*

*in alignment with the soul*
*it moves us to the 'place'*
*of the Beholder*
*who sees the self and the Self*
*enjoined in all aspects of life*

*behold the sun, dear one,*
*shining upon you*
*as you stand on Mother Earth…*

*be the blessed sun*
*that shines upon you*
*and breathe into the expansion*
*of Divine Love that you are…*

*you are both the sun itself*
*and the receiver of its warmth…*

*envision your life*
*however you choose…*

*you are the Beholder…*
*the creator…*
*the Divine Love that experiences all*

## *TIMELESSNESS*

*have you ever experienced joy?*

*you may notice in joy*
*that the concept of time leaves you*


*in a state of joy*
*timelessness is experienced…*

*twirling energies within*
*expand your being into brilliant light*
*that must….of its nature…*
*expand outward*
*in all directions*

*in such a state*
*time is no more*

*illusion is shattered*

*and the NOW becomes*
*the only Reality*

### SELF-LOVE

love your Self…

the Self that exists
beyond the world of form

**Self-love is truly this:**

**loving that which you are
unconditionally…**

**YOU ARE…**
that which transcends
time and space…and

knows Itself to be One with all Life…

to be One with the Father

who is LOVE

when you know deeply
this truth:

**only Love is real**

concerns for worldly matters
fall away

and your only thought
becomes…

where can I extend love now

*in this way,*

*you extend love*

*to the very Self you are*

## LOVE SPEAKS

*Love speaks to me in every moment*

*it welcomes me to the world*
*i have created…*

*while in this world*
*I remember I am Love*
*and all I see…all I experience*
*are my creations brought forth in Love*

*appearances tell me nothing*
*of the Truth*

*it is what I can see beyond the veil*
*that brings Love's message to me*

*my trust lies fully*
*in the One who Knows…*

*the One breathing life thru this body*
*extending outward…*
*to express and experience Itself…*
*in  **f e e l i n g***
*its very expression*
*thru e-motion*

*Love… desiring to know Itself…*
*moves in… with… and thru me*
*delighting in all It sees and embraces*

*and I am lifted up in the arms of Love*
*as I embrace all*
*with the loving eyes of Christ.*

### ALL WE BE
### to Michael and Denisa

softly.....lightly....
as grains of sand
moved by a gentle breeze.....

the blending of our voices
the sharing of our hearts
the expression of Jeshua energies...

Christ consciousness
is birthed thru us
as we create, explore, extend love
with and thru each other

the merging of identities
into the One Mind
releases us from
the illusion of separation

we are called to let go
of all remaining vestiges
of the small self
as we look to Oneness
for the Truth

old beliefs are repeatedly shaken
by this act of union...

long held perceptions crumble
as new eyes peer out
at a picture emerging
from a loving waterfall of colors

*One voice…..……..*

*………one heart…..*

*………………....…..one mind….*

*is all I see………..*

*……………is all we be*

## *COMING HOME*

*and now....we come home*

*to the Light that we are*

*to pass thru the eye of the needle*

*is to know only Oneness*

*no names.........*

*no identities..............*

*.........only Oneness*

## *ABOUT THE AUTHOR*

*In 2004, Anne DiDomenico left a corporate job to follow her spirit in a new way. This included realizing her deep desire to express to others her idea of the emerging Self... a presence she had developed a conscious awareness of early in her life. In the fall of 2006, Anne went into seclusion to find her voice. During this time, she experienced insights that allowed her to open to a fuller personal understanding of life events and her true God identity.*

*Between 2007 and 2008, Anne met Michael Carluccio and Denisa Nelson, and together, they co-authored three books:* The Bridge To Home: A Shortened Version of A Course in Miracles and The Way of Mastery, The Power of Jeshua Energies *and* Claiming Your Divinity: As Christ Walking Our World.

*Anne has written articles on mediation, conflict resolution and worldviews accessible at www.mediate.com. This is her first publishing effort in book form. Currently, Anne spends her time writing and coaching. She and her husband, Les, reside on the east coast surrounded by their son, Chad, grandchildren and an extended loving family circle. She may be reached at anne@emergeconsultingllc.com.*

2778768

Made in the USA